Dinosaurs of the Jurassic World and Beyond

DINOSAURS OF THE JURASSIC WORLD AND BEYOND

PAULA HAMMOND

SCHOLASTIC

www.scholastic.com

This edition published by Scholastic Inc., 557 Broadway, New York, NY 10012 by arrangement with Amber Books Ltd.

Scholastic Canada Ltd., Markham, Ontario
Scholastic Australia Pty. Ltd, Gosford NSW
Scholastic New Zealand Ltd., Greenmount, Auckland
Scholastic UK, Coventry, Warwickshire
Grolier International, Inc., Makati City, Philippines

1 2 3 4 5 6 7 8 9 10

ISBN: 978-0-545-85960-8

Editorial and design by
Amber Books Ltd
74–77 White Lion Street
London N1 9PF
United Kingdom
www.amberbooks.co.uk

Project Editor: Sarah Uttridge
Design: Keren Harragan

Printed in Shenzhen, China

Picture Credits:
All illustrations © IMP AB

Contents

Introduction

Once upon a time… Isn't that how the best stories always start?

Well, once upon a time—around 3.8 billion years ago—life on planet Earth began. It started on a small scale, with bacteria and single-celled microorganisms. Around 550 million years ago, fungi, jellies, sponges, and corals began to appear. Then, 485 million years ago, animals with backbones and jaws started to develop.

Now the story starts to really get going. In another 122 million years, the Earth would begin to look familiar. Soon fish would be jumping, insects would be buzzing, and odd-looking animals would be prowling across the landscape.

However, if the story of life on Earth was a book, then it would be a really big one! So big that it would be divided into chapters with names like Triassic and Jurassic Period. In each of these chapters—which are really periods of time—you would meet new, exciting characters. The story would even have its own monsters: armored fish, flying reptiles, and the "terrible lizards"—the dinosaurs.

Here, we will look at just some of the chapters from this tale and at the big and little monsters, from the Jurassic and beyond, that once called Earth home.

Dunkleosteus

(Dunk-lee-OH-stee-us)

Long before the dinosaurs, it was creatures like Dunkleosteus who ruled the Earth. This mighty armored fish was as big as a great white shark. It could flip its jaws open so quickly that its prey was literally sucked into its mouth.

▶ Dunkleosteus's jaws were the most powerful of any known creature. Sharp, bony plates acted like teeth, making this fish a top predator.

How big is it?

Did you know?

• At 33 ft. (10 m) long, Dunkleosteus was probably the largest fish of the Devonian Period.

• Dunkleosteus was named for David Dunkle, curator of vertebrate paleontology at the Cleveland Museum of Natural History.

Dimetrodon

 (Dy-MEE-tro-don)

Around 280 million years ago, this muscular monster made its home in the reed beds of what would become modern-day Texas. By raising its bulky body up on its squat legs, Dimetrodon could run down prey, a bit like a super-powered crocodile.

▶ Was its sail a way to attract a mate or a solar panel to warm its huge body? This is what scientists often ask about Dimetrodon.

How big is it?

Did you know?

• Although Dimetrodon looks like a dinosaur, it was actually a synapsid. These are reptiles that look like mammals.

• Dimetrodon means "two shapes of teeth." It had pointed canine teeth as well as smaller teeth that were shaped like teardrops.

Cynognathus

(Sy-nog-NAY-thus)

The name Cynognathus (which means "dog jaw") gives us a clue as to what this terror from the Triassic would have looked like. This successful and widespread hunter looked a bit like a wolf, with a huge head and jaws to match.

▶ One of these beasts would be dangerous, but just imagine Cynognathus hunting as part of a pack! It would have been terrifying!

How big is it?

Did you know?

• Mammals' legs are straight under their bodies, while lizards' legs splay out to the sides.

• Cynognathus's back legs were straight. Its front legs were splayed out, so it would have waddled as it ran.

Gracilisuchus

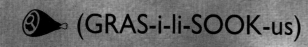 (GRAS-i-li-SOOK-us)

When its bones were first found in 1972, this long-tailed mini-reptile was thought to be a dinosaur. We now know that it is a type of pseudosuchia ("false crocodile"). These ancestors of crocodiles hunted in South America's steamy swamps.

▶ The secret to success is flexibility. Gracilisuchus hunted both on land and in shallow water. It also scavenged for food.

How big is it?

Did you know?

• •

• **Most scientific names come from Latin and Greek. Gracilisuchus is Latin for "graceful" and Greek for "crocodile."**

• **Although Gracilisuchus ran on all fours, it could also stand up on its powerful back legs.**

Scelidosaurus

 (SKEL-eye-doh-SAWR-us)

Scelidosaurus was a Jurassic-era eating machine. It had massive molar teeth for grinding up vegetation, and a large gut to process its food. Like the modern-day rhino, this dinosaur was a vegetarian, but he was no pushover.

▶ Scelidosaurus is one of the oldest thyreophorans (armored dinosaurs). Also in this group are the Ankylosauria and Stegosauria.

How big is it?

Scelidosaurus

Stegosaurus

Ankylosaurus

Did you know?

• •

• **Dinosaur names usually describe the creature's appearance. Scelidosaurus means "limb lizard" because of its powerful legs.**

• **Scelidosaurus was both big and tough. Its skin was covered in rows of oval scales called scutes.**

Megalosaurus

(MEG-ah-lo-SAWR-us)

Europe's Megalosaurus certainly lived up to its name, which means "big lizard." It measured around 30 ft. (9.1 m) long and 10 ft. (3 m) tall. Its weapons included sharp claws and killer teeth. Running on two legs, it was fast and smart.

▶ A cunning hunter knows that sick or old animals make easy pickings—even if that animal is an elephant-sized sauropod!

How big is it?

Did you know?

• •

• A Megalosaurus thighbone that was found in 1676 was believed to be the remains of a giant.

• In 1824, Megalosaurus became the first dinosaur to be validly named—148 years after its discovery!

Ophthalmosaurus

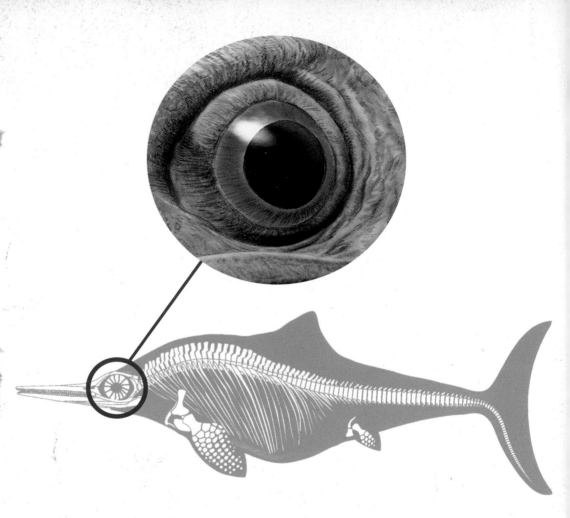

(Off-THAL-moh-SAWR-us)

Ophthalmosaurus means "eye lizard," and it's easy to see why this amazing creature earned its name. This great hunter had the biggest eye-to-body size of any known animal. It put its huge eyes to good use, looking for food in the deep, dark seas.

▶ This animal's eyes measured 4 in. (10.2 cm) across. Rings of bone around each eye protected them from pressure during deep dives.

How big is it?

Did you know?

• Ophthalmosaurus was an ichthyosaur. Ichthyosaurs were marine reptiles, which means they lived in salt water.

• Only the giant squid, which is much larger than Ophthalmosaurus, has eyes of a similar size.

Eustreptospondylus

(You-STREP-to-SPON-die-lus)

Say the word "dinosaur" and most of us imagine a meat-eating monster like Eustreptospondylus. It had powerful back legs, tiny forearms, and massive jaws. It hunted on the shores of southern England, eating smaller dinosaurs and reptiles.

▶ Disaster strikes! Or does it? Just like today's Komodo dragons, Eustreptospondylus could probably swim for short distances.

How big is it?

Did you know?

• •

• **Eustreptospondylus belongs to the same family —and looks similar to—** *Tyrannosaurus rex.*

• **Its name means "true Streptospondylus." A Streptospondylus is a type of theropod. These were two-legged meat-eating dinosaurs.**

Allosaurus

 (Al-oh-SAWR-us)

Allosaurus is one of the most famous and well-researched dinosaurs; it has been a star of the big and small screen. It grew up to 39 ft. (11.9 m) in length and could live for about 28 years. The name of this mighty carnivore means "different lizard."

▶ Young sauropods made the perfect target for Allosaurus. Its saw-like teeth allowed it to slice flesh off its victims with ease.

How big is it?

Did you know?

• Two almost complete Allosaurus fossils that were found in **Wyoming** were named **Big Al** and **Big Al Two**.

• The **BBC** Television show "The Ballad of Big Al" imagined the theropod's life and death.

Kentrosaurus

 (KEN-troh-SAWR-us)

Armed with bristling spines, this late Jurassic stegosaurian had little to fear from predators. It lived in what is now East Africa, and shared the hot, tropical Earth with theropods like Allosaurus, ancient sharks, crocodiles, and small mammals.

▶ Kentrosaurus's spines and spear-loaded tail make formidable weapons—as this would-be attacker has just found out!

How big is it?

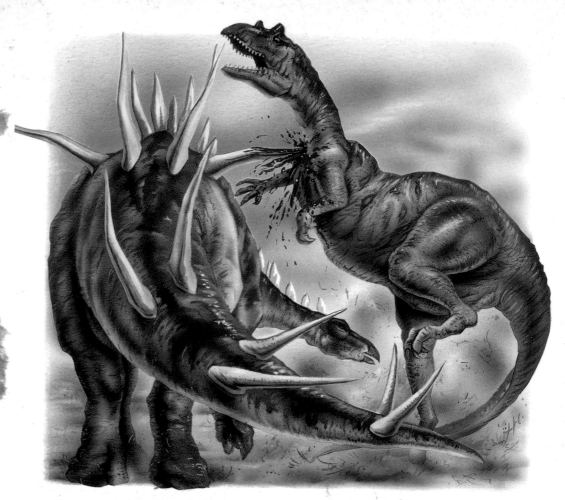

Did you know?

• Kentrosaurus's tail could move through a full 180 degrees, and reach whiplash speeds of 31 mph (50 kph).

• Kentrosaurus means "pointed-tail saurian." Saurian is the scientific name for reptiles like lizards and crocodiles.

Stegosaurus

 (STEG-oh-SAWR-us)

This gigantic "roofed lizard" was as big as a bus, with a brain the size of a bent hot dog! But what Stegosaurus lacked in brains it made up for in size and strength. It was heavily armored and moved with the power and grace of an elephant.

▶ An adult Stegosaurus could be dangerous. Allosaurus fossils have been found with wounds matching Stegosaurus' tail spikes.

How big is it?

Did you know?

• Rows of heat-controlling plates along this dinosaur's back may have changed color during mating displays.

• In the *Far Side* comic, cavemen called the Stegosaurus tail spikes "thagomizers." Paleontologists now use this term, too!

Apatosaurus

🌿 (Uh-PAT-uh-SAWR-us)

"Deceptive lizard" is a good name for this dinosaur! During the 1870s, scientists eager to make new finds identified the immature and adult bones of this dinosaur as two separate species: Apatosaurus and Brontosaurus. Confusion followed.

▶ Apatosaurus belongs to a family of four-legged vegetarian dinosaurs that includes some of the longest creatures the Earth has ever seen.

How big is it?

Did you know?

• •

• **Diplodocids such as Apatosaurus could whip-snap their very long tails to generate a deafening sonic boom!**

• **Apatosaurus is still sometimes called Brontosaurus. In 1989, the U.S. Post Office even issued a stamp featuring Brontosaurus.**

Archaeopteryx

 (Ark-ee-OP-ter-icks)

Europe was a group of tropical islands 150 million years ago. This is where Archaeopteryx lived, gliding from island to island to hunt. This animal is a link between dinosaurs and birds. It had razor-sharp teeth, a long bony tail, and feathers.

▶ Archaeopteryx had an **extra-long toe,** known as a killing claw. It probably fed on insects and small lizards.

How big is it?

Did you know?

• **Archaeopteryx means "ancient feather."** This creature is also sometimes called Urvogel, which is German for "original bird."

• **Aurornis ("dawn bird") was an animal that lived 10 million years earlier than Archaeopteryx, but probably could not fly.**

Baryonyx

(Bare-ee-ON-iks)

Meat-eaters like Baryonyx were top predators around the great lakes that covered Northern Europe 130 million years ago. With a narrow snout like a crocodile and claws that were shaped like fishermen's gaffs, Baryonyx was great at catching fish.

▶ Standing on the water's edge, Baryonyx uses its long claws to sweep fish from the water into its waiting jaws.

How big is it?

Did you know?

• Baryonyx means "heavy claw." These fearsome claws measured 9.8 in. (25 cm) long. This creature's teeth were serrated (saw-edged).

• Baryonyx had an upper jaw that sloped down toward its snout to stop fish from wriggling free.

Iguanodon

 (Ig-WAHN-oh-don)

Iguanodon was a success story of the Early Cretaceous. It could walk on four legs, or rise up on two legs when grazing. These dinosaurs also had replaceable teeth, a bony "beak" for cropping tough vegetation, and flexible little fingers for handling food.

▶ A pair of wicked spikes in place of thumbs gave this formidable vegetarian a huge advantage in the fight for survival!

How big is it?

Did you know?

• •

• **When Iguanodon ("iguana-tooth") bones were first discovered, this dinosaur's thumb spike was thought to be a horn that grew out of its nose.**

• **Iguanodon could walk on two legs ("bipedal") or on four legs ("quadrupedal"). It became more quadrupedal as it grew older.**

Utahraptor

 (YOU-ta-RAP-tor)

In 1991, paleontologists were very excited when a gigantic claw was found in Gaston Quarry in Utah. This dinosaur, called "Utah's predator," was the largest raptor ever discovered. These scary hunters used their curved claws to disembowel prey.

▶ Working as a team, the raptors circle their prey. They separate the weakest members of the herd before moving in for the attack.

How big is it?

Did you know?

- Some paleontologists believe that Utahraptor was covered in feathers and warm-blooded, just like a mammal today.

- Some people wanted to call Utahraptor *Utahraptor spielbergi* after the film director Steven Spielberg, who made *Jurassic Park*.

Giganotosaurus

(JY-gan-ot-oh-SAWR-us)

Giganotosaurus' name means "great Southern lizard." It was an enormous hunter that lived in what is now modern-day Argentina. It weighed up to 30,420 lb (13.8 tonnes). This two-legged dinosaur was big, bad, and dangerous!

▶ To tackle herd animals like Argentinosaurus, Giganotosaurus may have hunted in packs or, if fresh food was scarce, scavenged corpses.

How big is it?

Did you know?

· ·

• **Giganotosaurus had a top speed of 31 mph (50 kph). If it had gone any faster it would have toppled over.**

• ***Giganotosaurus carolinii* was named after the amateur fossil hunter, Ruben Carolini, who discovered it.**

Pteranodon

 (Ter-ANN-uh-don)

For four million years, these magnificent pterosaurs dominated the skies over land that, today, we call North America. These flying reptiles nested in colonies on sea cliffs, and spent long periods soaring over the warm waters in search of food.

▶ Pteranodon lived 86–84 million years ago. The oldest known pterosaur, Eudimorphodon, lived 210–203 million years ago.

How big is it?

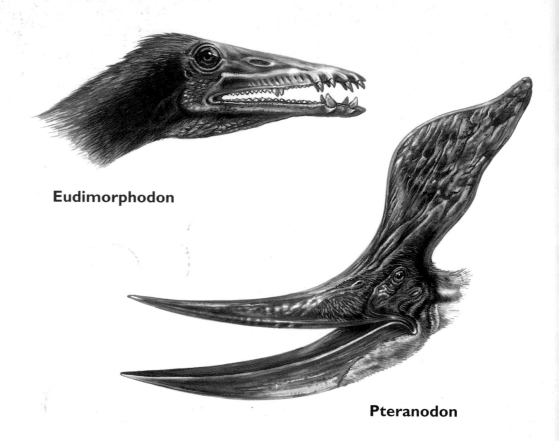

Eudimorphodon

Pteranodon

Did you know?

• •

• **Pteranodon (which means "toothless wing") was not a dinosaur, despite appearing in many movies and books about dinosaurs.**

• **Although it did not have feathers, Pteranodon's long, tapering wings were similar to those of seabirds like the albatross.**

Hesperornis

 (hess-puh-RAWR-nihs)

This flightless, aquatic bird looked a bit like modern birds such as grebes. When it was found, it helped scientists understand how dinosaurs evolved into birds. Hesperornis (which means "western bird") was a superb diver and skilled fisher.

▶ A long, pointed bill, lined with needle-sharp teeth, makes a perfect weapon for catching fish and keeping hold of slippery prey.

How big is it?

Did you know?

. . . .

• Hesperornis was so well adapted for life at sea that it probably struggled to walk on land.

• Some people think that Hesperornis would have pushed itself along on its belly, like penguins do now.

Edmontonia

 (Ed-mon-TONE-ee-uh)

Edmontonia was built like a tank. It looked like a cross between a giant aardvark and a crocodile. It had a wide body protected by flat armored plates. Its other weapons included dagger-style spikes and a bony, whip-like tail.

▶ Whether they were used in battles between males for mates, or to defend Edmontonia from predators, these spikes were deadly.

How big is it?

Did you know?

• •

• Its name comes from the Edmonton Formation, Canada, where the first fossils were discovered.

• Edmontonia is the "genus" name. At least three different species are known within this group.

Styracosaurus

(Sty-ra-co-SAWR-us)

Styracosaurus's neck frill was its most valuable asset. This huge, bony neck plate protected Styracosaurus in combat. Like a peacock's tail feathers, it also made this monstrous beast look even more impressive to potential mates.

▶ The most dangerous beast in modern Africa is not the lion but the rhinoceros. Styracosaurus was probably just as deadly!

How big is it?

Did you know?

• Styracosaurus's teeth were continually replaced, as they were worn out by chewing on tough, low-lying vegetation.

• Styracosaurus means "spiked lizard." In Ancient Greek, a styrax was a type of spear.

Velociraptor

 (Vel-OSS-ih-RAP-tor)

Velociraptor is probably one of the world's most famous dinosaurs. After being featured in the "Jurassic Park" series of movies, this fast and fearsome raptor became one of paleontology's most well-known killers.

▶ A retractable claw that was 3.5 in. (9 cm) long on each foot was used to pierce through the tough skin of this monster's prey.

How big is it?

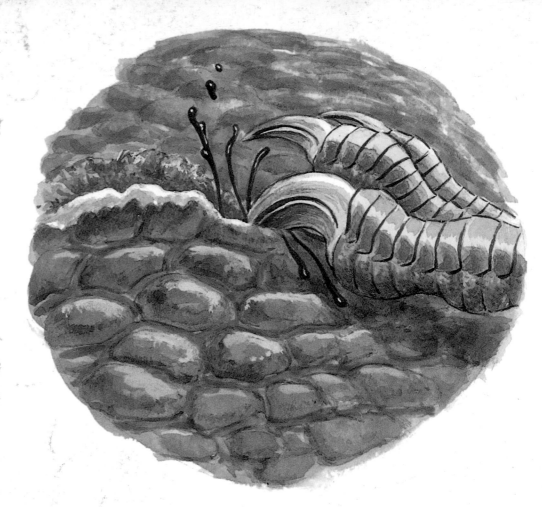

Did you know?

• **Velociraptor ancestors, Rahonavis, could fly. Velociraptor kept its feathery coat but lost its ability to fly.**

• **Like birds, Velociraptor (whose name means "swift predator") also had hollow bones and laid nests of eggs.**

Tyrannosaurus

(Ty-RAN-oh-sawr-us)

When western North America was an island, 68 million years ago, Tyrannosaurus ruled the land. The mightiest of this group of clawed dinosaurs was Tyrannosaurus rex. Growing up to 40 ft. (12.2 m) long, T. rex was one of the world's largest land carnivores.

▶ Birds evolved from small theropod dinosaurs. Scientists think that T. rex is related to alligators, chickens, and ostriches!

How big is it?

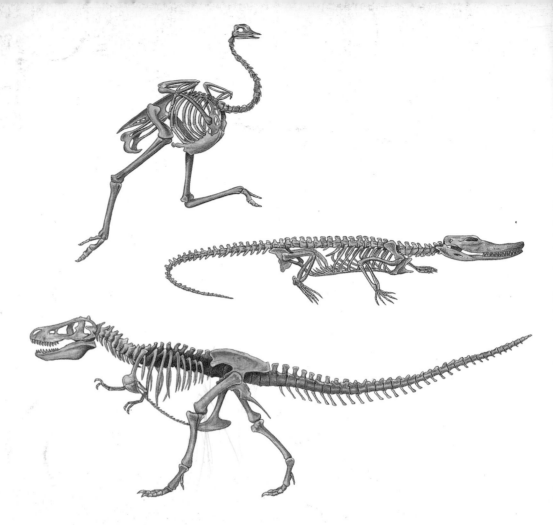

Did you know?

• **Chicago's Field Museum of Natural History owns the largest and most complete specimen of a Tyrannosaurus, which is nicknamed Sue.**

• **Tyrannosaurus means "tyrant lizard." Rex is Latin for "king," which makes T. rex the king of the tyrannosaurids.**

Triceratops

 (Try-SER-a-tops)

Three scary horns give this North American dinosaur its scientific name: "three horn face." These horns and frilled neck plate may have been used for protection or used in mating displays, but scientists are not quite sure.

▶ All ceratopsian dinosaurs had horns and bony frills that came in many shapes and sizes. Styracosaurus (page 48) is another one.

How big is it?

Did you know?

• •

• **Fossilized dung from a T. rex was found to contain bones from the frill of a Triceratops.**

• **Scientists used to think that fossilized Triceratops bones belonged to an extinct species of buffalo.**

Andrewsarchus

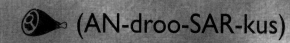 (AN-droo-SAR-kus)

An asteroid strike 66 million years ago wiped out 75 percent of life on Earth. The K–Pg Extinction Event meant the end of the dinosaurs but gave new species the chance to develop. The hyena-like Andrewsarchus was one of those.

▶ Only Andrewsarchus's skull has been found. However, we can guess that, like many mammals, it both hunted and scavenged for food.

How big is it?

Did you know?

· ·

• **Andrewsarchus's skull measured about twice the length of that of a modern-day brown bear.**

• **Studies suggest that Andrewsarchus had some of the strongest jaws ever seen on a land mammal.**

Megalodon

(MEG-a-lo-don)

Dinosaurs may have been dead, but the world of the Pliocene still had its share of giants. Growing up to 59 ft. (18 m) long, this ancient shark was an adaptable hunter, equally at home seeking prey in shallow lagoons or in warm oceans.

▶ Fossils suggest that Megalodon feasted on fish, turtles, and a wide range of marine mammals such as whales, porpoises, and sea lions.

How big is it?

Did you know?

• **Megalodon teeth were once believed to be dragon tongues that had been petrified (turned to stone).**

• **Megalodon probably died out as a result of the Earth cooling and the sea levels falling.**

Smilodon

 (SMILE-oh-don)

Back when the Americas were covered in lush forests, this sabre-toothed cat was a king of the jungle. Preying on large mammals such as camels, horses, and bison, only one predator was more dangerous—the newly arrived human!

▶ Whether used for slashing or stabbing, Smilodon's 11 in. (28 cm) fangs would have made short work of a Woolly Mammoth.

How big is it?

Did you know?

· ·

• Smilodon (which means "knife tooth") lived 2.5 million–10,000 years ago. It died out during the Quaternary Extinction Event.

• Smilodon remains found in the La Brea Tar Pits in Los Angeles probably came from animals that were trapped in tar while scavenging.

Woolly Mammoth

 (WUH-lee-MAM-uth)

Cave paintings made 11,000 years ago prove that our ancestors both admired and hunted these creatures. Similar to modern elephants in shape and size, they were found in Europe, North Asia, and North America during the last Ice Age.

▶ Neanderthals used mammoth bones to build huts and make tools. But were humans responsible for the mammoth's extinction?

How big is it?

Did you know?

• **Often when animals are fossilized, their flesh and bone are replaced by mud and minerals.**

• **Mammoths (meaning "big") that are found frozen in deep ice could contain material that could be used to create clones!**

Index

Key

. . . .

 Mainly feeds on other animals

 Mainly eats fish

 Mainly eats plants